TOULOUSE-LAUTREC

The Moulin Rouge and the City of Light

ROBERT BURLEIGH

Published in association with The Art Institute of Chicago

Harry N. Abrams, Inc.

Toulouse-Lautrec
in his studio, painting
*Training of the New Girls
by Valentin le Désossé.*

Paris, France, 1891. A small bearded man sits at a table in the shadowy corner of a crowded dance hall. He holds in his hands a sketchbook and a pencil. He leans forward, peering intently at the stage through thin-framed spectacles. Women wearing lace, feathers, and frills twirl past, kicking their legs high into the air. Music vibrates off the walls. Mirrors flicker. Customers call out. The huge room glows with a greenish-white light.

But the man is not performing, shouting, or dancing like the others. No, he is watching.

His pencil moves quickly. He wants to capture the swirl and joy of this moment. He will use these sketches later, when he returns to his studio to paint. He will bring this colorful world to life again on paper, cardboard, and canvas—and it will remain alive for us, so many years later, when we look at his work.

WHO IS THIS MAN?

HE IS HENRI DE TOULOUSE-LAUTREC . . . .

Or, to be exact: Henri Marie-Raymond de Toulouse-Lautrec Monfa. If that strikes you as the fancy name of a nobleman, you are right. The Toulouse-Lautrec family owned much property in the south of France and traced its ancestry back hundreds of years. The family was even related to a man who claimed to be the French king. In 1864, when Henri was born, his future looked bright.

Training of the New Girls by Valentin le Désossé, 1889–90, oil on canvas, 45 1/4 x 59 inches.

Henri de Toulouse-Lautrec at around age two.

Baby Henri—nicknamed "Little Jewel" by his parents—entered a privileged world of traveling, hunting, sailing, and horseback riding. His father and uncles were excellent amateur artists, and Henri inherited their talents. Lively pencil drawings of animals—done when he was just a boy and a young teenager—catch a feeling of movement that would become a characteristic of his adult style.

Henri was a likeable, happy child. Would he follow the path of his dashing father, a sportsman who loved parties and delighted in dressing up in odd costumes? Most people thought so. But then Henri's life took a strange, cruel twist.

At age thirteen, he fell while getting up from a chair, breaking his left leg. Just over a year later, he stumbled and broke the other leg. It turned out that he suffered from a disease that left him with, among other things, weakened bones; his recovery was slow—and incomplete. Henri's upper body continued to grow; but his legs remained those of a little boy. As an adult, he would be less than five feet tall.

At first, Henri despaired. And yet his cheerful disposition and a renewed interest in art gave him hope. During his long recovery, he drew more and more. Unable to move about, he looked closely at what was around him—his father's horses, the woods surrounding the house, his pets, and the people who visited or worked on the estate. He began to paint what he saw.

Art mattered deeply to the young Lautrec. He realized that if he wanted to become an artist—a real artist—he would have to study in Paris, where all the best teachers and art schools were. Was that possible?

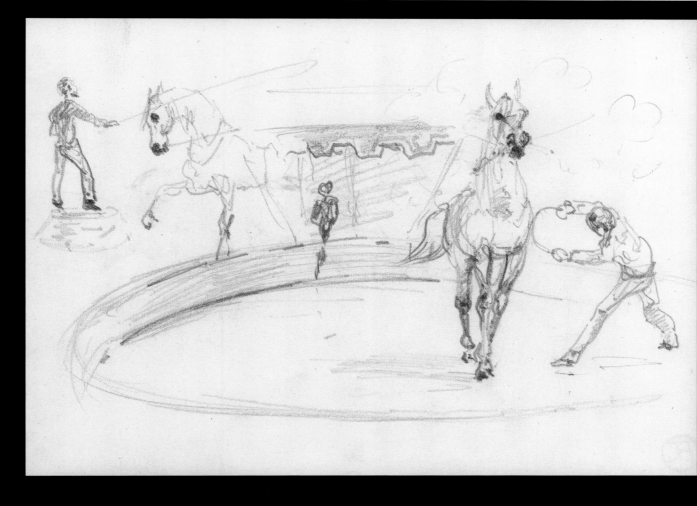

As a teenager, Henri was taken by his mother to Nice, a seaside resort town in the south of France. He brought along a sketchbook in which he drew scenes from the world around him. The drawings show his early talent for capturing people and animals, especially horses, in motion.

In the early 1880s, Paris was not only the capital of France; it was, in truth, "the capital of pleasure for the whole Western world." The glamour and brilliance of newly installed electric lights symbolized a new age, one of modern technologies and exciting nightlife. Beautiful, glittering Paris—City of Light. It beckoned. Lautrec answered its call.

IN 1882 HE EMBARKED ON THE GREAT ADVENTURE OF HIS LIFE.

Lautrec's father and mother agreed to his art studies reluctantly. They believed an art-making career was not appropriate for a person of his wealth and status. Perhaps because of his family's disapproval, Lautrec sometimes signed his work with a variety of names. One such made-up name, or pseudonym, was "Tréclau." It consists of the letters that make up the name "Lautrec."

His fellow students in Paris included a number of people who would one day become famous artists. The most notable was Vincent van Gogh, whose portrait Lautrec painted in 1887. He and van Gogh became good friends.

Lautrec worked hard. His drawing and painting continued to improve. He also studied the work of other artists, such as the Impressionists. They painted scenes from everyday life, capturing light and light's reflections with short, rapid brushstrokes.

Top Left: *The Place du Havre, Paris*, 1893, by Camille Pissarro, oil on canvas, 23 5/8 x 28 13/16 inches; **Bottom Left:** *Dance at the Moulin de la Galette, Montmartre*, 1876, by Auguste Renoir, oil on canvas, 51 5/8 x 68 7/8 inches. These two Impressionist paintings show the vibrant daily life of Paris at the end of the nineteenth century.

Lautrec as a young adult.

Student life, however, was more than work and study. Lautrec, with his crippled legs, lisp, and, according to some, slightly deformed facial features, might well have become a loner. Not Henri! He made friends easily. He charmed them with his wit, his varied interests, and his warm, brown-eyed gaze. They no doubt appreciated his generosity, too. He was well known for his lavish dinner parties.

Central Paris was a city of wide, tree-lined, shop-filled avenues, where the well-to-do promenaded or rode in horse-drawn carriages. But there were other sides to Paris—and Lautrec and his artist friends found them.

Montmartre, a former village set on a high hill, was now a part of Paris. It was a district of narrow streets, cheap housing, and inexpensive restaurants. It soon became the destination of many struggling artists and writers.

THERE WAS SOMETHING ELSE

IN MONTMARTRE, TOO . . .

457. – PARIS. – Un Coin du Vieux Montmartre

Postcard of a corner of old Montmartre.

... THE WORLD
OF THE NIGHT.

Lautrec and his friends became regulars at the music halls, vaudeville shows, and cabarets, where dancers, singers, and storytellers competed with more exotic forms of entertainment such as boxing kangaroos. An evening might even conclude with a costume party!

Two of the best-known music halls in Montmartre were the Chat Noir (the Black Cat) and the Moulin Rouge (the Red Mill). The Moulin Rouge (which Lautrec went to so often that he had a table permanently reserved for him) was in a district dotted with what had once been grain mills. A huge, lit-up mill wheel turned in the darkness above the music hall's roof, dazzling like a sky full of spinning stars.

HERE, ALL KINDS OF PEOPLE MINGLED:
ARTISTS LIKE LAUTREC
WORKERS ON THEIR DAY OFF,
MIDDLE-CLASS PEOPLE LOOKING FOR
A NIGHT OF ADVENTURE

even rich aristocrats excited by a side of Paris they didn't usually see. Everyone loved the nightlife in Montmartre! And no one more than Henri de Toulouse-Lautrec. The place and its people were about to become the focus of his life and art.

The Moulin Rouge.

At the Circus Fernando: Medrano with a Piglet, c. 1889, oil on paper laid down on board, 22 x 14 1/2 inches.

Given Lautrec's busy social life, one might think he made very little art. But the opposite is true. In the fifteen years from 1886 to his death in 1901,

HE COMPLETED OVER 725 OIL PAINTINGS, 275 WATERCOLORS,

MORE THAN 325 PRINTS AND POSTERS,

AND AROUND 5,000 DRAWINGS.

Lautrec created his first important large painting around 1887 or 1888. In *Equestrienne* (*At the Circus Fernando*), a horse and rider gallop around the ring of the circus as the ringmaster snaps his whip. The white circle at the top of the painting is actually a paper hoop being held by a clown (you can see his striped socks and puffy pants). In a moment the rider will leap off of the horse and burst through the paper, landing on the animal on the other side!

Equestrienne (At the Circus Fernando), 1887–88, oil on canvas, 39 1/2 x 63 1/2 inches. In this painting the people watching the circus are barely visible. Lautrec focused on the action in the ring. As always, he loved to portray people and animals in motion. The paint seems brushed on quickly, to create a sense of rapid movement.

A printing factory in Paris, showing rotary presses used to make color posters.

Lautrec's career was soon to take off. This was not due to his painting, but to another art form—the advertising poster. Remember: It was a time before radio, television, and film. To spread word about the performers of the day, the cabarets used huge, brightly colored posters. Such posters, hung on walls throughout Paris, were sometimes called "the art of the streets." And Lautrec was at the forefront of this movement.

Dancers from the Moulin Rouge. La Goulue is doing a split.

In 1891 he made a poster for the Moulin Rouge. And why not? He frequented the cabaret, he knew its entertainers, and he was a painter whose skills were already well known. The result was a poster that in many ways revolutionized this art form. Its title is *Moulin Rouge, La Goulue*, the name of the high-kicking woman at the poster's center.

Moulin Rouge, La Goulue, 1891, lithograph, 75 1/4 x 46 inches. La Goulue was an energetic dancer named for her large appetite (which is what her nickname means in French) and her rather coarse language. Part of her act included kicking off the top hat of one of the enthralled spectators! Her partner was the shadowy figure in the poster's foreground, Valentin le Désossé (the Boneless), known for his amazing flexibility.

Yvette Guilbert Singing, c. 1894, graphite on paper, 13 1/8 x 8 1/16 inches.

The poster is extremely large—nearly six feet high—and printed on three sheets of paper. About three thousand copies appeared on walls throughout Paris. People loved them so much they began peeling them off the walls and bringing them home.

The Moulin Rouge poster helped La Goulue—along with Lautrec—become a star. Other entertainers wanted Lautrec to make posters featuring them. Lautrec tended to focus his attention on one celebrity at a time. He would create many drawings, paintings, and posters of one person before moving on to someone else. Once, intrigued by an actress playing in Paris, he saw her perform in the same play twenty times!

One famous Lautrec subject was Yvette Guilbert, a tall, black-gloved "singer," who spoke, more than sang, her songs.

LAUTREC WAS DRAWN TO THE QUALITIES
THAT MADE EACH PERSON DISTINCTIVE.

Thus his drawings and posters of Guilbert often featured her long neck and sharp nose, exaggerated to the point of caricature. He even used the black gloves by themselves to represent Guilbert. If you look hard at his poster called *Divan Japonais*, you may be able to find Guilbert (or at least her gloves!) at the very top.

16

Divan Japonais, 1893, lithograph, 31 5/8 x 24 3/8 inches.

Jane Avril, 1893, lithograph, 50 3/4 x 37 inches. In this image of Jane Avril, Lautrec emphasizes the dancer's large, distinctive bonnet, which she also wears in the photograph opposite.

Jane Avril doing one of her famous splits.

Lautrec also made poster portraits of his good friend Jane Avril, a dancer who specialized in "splits" and the "military salute" (in which she held one leg over her head).

AVRIL'S WILD DANCE STYLE EARNED HER THE NICKNAME "LA MELINITE," THE FRENCH WORD FOR A FORM OF DYNAMITE.

Perhaps the most famous of all Lautrec's subjects was the poet-singer Aristide Bruant. Bruant wrote and sang songs about social outcasts that challenged the safe, stuffy lives of wealthy French people.

19

Left: Aristide Bruant; **Right:** *The Actor Namakura Sukegorō II,* 1768, by Katsukawa Shunshō, woodblock print, 12 13/16 x 5 7/8 inches; **Opposite:** *Aristide Bruant, in His Cabaret,* 1893, lithograph, 54 3/8 x 39 inches. Both Lautrec's poster and the Japanese print show famous performers. They also both use the same colors and even some of the same shapes.

Lautrec's best-known poster of Bruant captures the poet's romantic flair. The portrayal of the scowling Bruant, in his wide-brimmed hat, red scarf, and black cloak, is one of the most famous entertainer images in the history of art. Bruant, for one, was impressed with the poster. "Am I really that grand?" he once asked Lautrec. "Even grander," Henri replied confidently. "That's what the future will say!"

The poster features a Lautrec specialty—broad, flat areas of color. Lautrec, along with many other French painters, was influenced in his use of color by Japanese art, which was then all the rage in Europe. For centuries, Japan had not allowed outsiders in. The country had opened its borders to the West only twenty-five years earlier, so it was still considered new and exciting. Lautrec himself collected Japanese prints.

A model poses for
a painting by Lautrec.

Friends who came to have their portraits painted were always sure of a good time. Sitting before his easel in his large felt hat, Lautrec would paint and tell stories, hum, or sing songs. Often, when the weather was pleasant, he suggested going for a walk rather than continuing with the portrait. One sitter remembers going to the studio several times a week for a month—but only sitting for a total of three hours.

Although Lautrec believed in "capturing the moment" (and his art seems to do just that), he frequently took a long time to construct his paintings. He made many sketches, used hired models and sometimes photographs, and also worked from memory.

This is especially true of his famous painting *At the Moulin Rouge*. It shows several groups of people mingling in the Montmartre cabaret.

THE PEOPLE SEATED AT THE TABLE
ARE ALL FRIENDS OF LAUTREC.

Jane Avril, with her bright red hair, sits with her back to us. Look carefully and you can see a small figure in the upper center walking beside a much taller man—it is Lautrec himself! La Goulue stands in the rear, gazing in a mirror as she fixes her distinctive bun. The face on the extreme right, half in, half out of the picture, belongs to Lautrec's dancer friend May Milton.

At the Moulin Rouge, 1892/95, oil on canvas, 48 7/16 x 55 1/2 inches.

May Milton, 1895, oil and pastel on cardboard, 26 x 19 1/2 inches.

We—the painting's viewers—look at this cast of characters. They in turn are looking at each other, or at us. Yet for the most part there is no eye contact. The Moulin Rouge patrons seem lost in thought. The whole scene captures the noisy, brightly lit atmosphere of the cabaret.

No one seems to be having great fun, and the greenish-white mask-like face on the right is almost frightening. Why Lautrec painted May Milton in this way is not exactly clear, but we know that he also painted her in a more lifelike way, as he did in a work on cardboard of around the same time.

If you don't like May Milton's spooky face, you're not alone. After Lautrec died, someone actually cut an L-shaped portion of canvas—including the face—off of the painting!

Nobody is sure who did this or why. Later the cut strip was sewn back onto the canvas. Maybe someone realized that the face, though strange, made the painting more unusual and interesting.

Photograph showing the L-shaped portion of canvas cut off of *At the Moulin Rouge*.

Later in the 1890s, Lautrec moved from his apartment in Montmartre to a more fashionable part of Paris. By this time, the fast pace of the Paris nightlife was taking its toll on his health and happiness. Friends tried to take him on short trips to get him out of the city. His parents eventually had him placed briefly in a hospital. Even there, he continued to make art. Painting and drawing from memory, he returned to one of his favorite themes—circus life—and impressed the doctors with his talent. Still, his health worsened.

On September 9, 1901, the spirited artist who would forever be identified with one of the most colorful periods in French history died. Henri de Toulouse-Lautrec was thirty-six years old.

Above: *At the Circus: Work in the Ring*, 1899, charcoal, pastel, black chalk, and colored pencil on paper, 8 1/2 x 12 7/16 inches; **Opposite:** *At the Circus: Trained Pony and Baboon*, c. 1899, pastel, pencil, and graphite on paper, 17 1/4 x 10 1/2 inches. Lautrec created these drawings while he was in the hospital. He returned to themes he had loved as a young child and student.

The Moulin Rouge still exists today. It continues to be a popular tourist destination, largely because Lautrec made it so famous.

But the end was not quite the end. If Henri de Toulouse-Lautrec did not live far into the twentieth century, his fame did. Lautrec's influence is enduring. His work has always been popular and he himself has become a kind of artistic hero. There are countless books and movies about him and the places he made famous—Montmartre and the Moulin Rouge.

For years painters have looked to his work for inspiration. Many artists have been encouraged by his boldness and realism in bringing the world of Montmartre to life. Stirred by Lautrec's vivid works, these artists have explored daring new subjects of their own.

A courageous human being, a fun-loving, witty man, and an immortal artist, Henri de Toulouse-Lautrec has surely left his mark on our times. As one of his friends said:

"TOULOUSE–LAUTREC—THE OFTENER YOU SEE HIM, THE TALLER HE GROWS."

Trick photograph of Henri de Toulouse-Lautrec as painter and model.

BIBLIOGRAPHY

A wall in Paris covered with posters. The poster at the top that reads "Aristide Bruant" was designed by Lautrec.

- Denvir, Bernard, *Toulouse-Lautrec*, Thames and Hudson, London, 1991

- Dortu, M. G., and Huisman, P., *Lautrec by Lautrec*, Viking Press, New York, 1964

- Robbins, Daniel and Eugenia S., *Henri de Toulouse-Lautrec*, Art Institute of Chicago, 1980

- Stuckey, Charles F., *Toulouse-Lautrec: Paintings*, Art Institute of Chicago, 1979

- Venezia, Mike, *Henri de Toulouse-Lautrec*, Children's Press, Chicago, 1995 (This is a short, easy-to-read introduction to Lautrec for very young children.)

ACKNOWLEDGMENTS

The author would like to thank the many people who made this book possible, especially Susan Rossen and Amanda Freymann of the Publications Department at the Art Institute of Chicago. Art Institute curator Mary Weaver Chapin was extremely helpful in working out the book's major themes and providing valuable information. Annie Feldmeier carefully organized the visual material, and Katie Reilly was indispensable in all phases of the book's development, from text revisions to visual selections. Thanks to all these individuals and also to my editor at Abrams Books for Young Readers, Howard Reeves.

AUTHOR'S NOTE

Reading about and writing about Toulouse-Lautrec was a great delight. My generalist's picture of Lautrec, largely taken from popular culture, was of a man rather embittered by life and lost in a fog of alcohol and decadence.

Instead, I found him a person who, despite his well-known physical limitations, was curious, open to life, witty, generous to his many friends, and, of course, extremely gifted. This book focuses on Lautrec as a painter of Paris nightlife and as one of the fathers of the poster; it does not emphasize his serious addiction to drink, which was certainly part of the picture.

Lautrec's exceptional creativity derived mainly from two things: an innate talent and a dedication to hard work. These attributes, particularly the latter, often get lost in the typical portrait of Lautrec as the embodiment of the nineteenth-century bohemian art world. The number of his completed artworks, the various genres he worked in, and his concern for getting it right could serve as an inspiration for any young artist and, indeed, for anyone trying to accomplish anything of value. I hope that this book captures the spirit of a remarkable man but also that it reminds readers of why we still remember Henri de Toulouse-Lautrec: He was a wonderful painter and draftsman whose works continue to fascinate and inspire.

The Simpson Chain, 1896, lithograph, 33 1/2 x 48 3/8 inches. In the later 1890s, Lautrec found another new interest: cycling. He had long had a passion for sports and loved to row, sail, and even swim. He was caught up in the French craze for this new sport. He made several posters and drawings of cyclists in motion.

TO FRANK ZIRBEL, ARTIST
—R. B.

Design by Celina Carvalho
Production Manager: Jonathan Lopes

Library of Congress Cataloging-in-Publication Data

Burleigh, Robert.
Toulouse-Lautrec : the Moulin Rouge and the city of light / Robert Burleigh.
p. cm.
ISBN 0-8109-5867-8
1. Toulouse-Lautrec, Henri de, 1864-1901—Juvenile literature. 2. Artists—France—Biography—Juvenile literature. I. Art Institute of Chicago. II. Title.

N6853.T6B87 2005
760'.092—dc22

2004023448

Printed and bound in China
1 3 5 7 9 10 8 6 4 2

▲

Harry N. Abrams, Inc.
100 Fifth Avenue, New York, NY 10011
www.abramsbooks.com
Abrams is a subsidiary of

LA MARTINIÈRE
GROUPE

ILLUSTRATION CREDITS

Unless stated otherwise in a caption, all artwork is by Henri de Toulouse-Lautrec. All photographs of objects in the collection of the Art Institute © The Art Institute of Chicago. Unless otherwise stated, all photographs of works of art appear by permission of the owners. Many of the images in this publication are protected by copyright and may not be available for further reproduction without consent of the copyright holder. Every effort has been made to contact copyright holders for all reproductions.

Front cover, title page, 15: The Art Institute of Chicago (AIC), The Mr. and Mrs. Carter H. Harrison Collection, 1954.1193. **2, 4:** Musée Toulouse-Lautrec, Albi, Tarn, France. **3:** The Philadelphia Museum of Art, The Henry P. McIlhenny Collection in memory of Frances P. McIlhenny, 1986.026.032. **5:** AIC, Robert Alexander Waller Memorial Fund, 1949.80. **6 top:** AIC, Potter Palmer Collection, 1922.434. **6 bottom:** Musée d'Orsay, Paris, France / Réunion des Musées Nationaux / Art Resource, NY. **8, 11, 29:** Getty Images / Collection Roger-Viollet, 690-9, 9447-10, 41-31. **9:** Photograph courtesy Galerie & Éditions Roussard, Montmartre, France. **12:** Anonymous loan to The Art Institute of Chicago, 314.1996. **13:** AIC, Joseph Winterbotham Collection, 1925.523. **14 top:** Marius Vachon, *Les Arts et les industries du papier en France* (Paris: Librairies-imprimeries réunies, 1894), p. 194. **14 bottom, 20 left, 22, back cover:** Getty Images / Harlingue / Roger-Viollet, 1577-10, 1179-7, 1179-73764-4. **16, 31:** AIC, promised gift of the Collection of Francey and Dr. Martin L. Gecht. **17, 18, 21, spine:** AIC, gift of Carter H. Harrison, 1949.1002, 1949.1004, 1949.1005. **19:** *Toulouse-Lautrec: Prints and Posters from the Bibliothèque Nationale* (Brisbane: Queensland Art Gallery, 1991), p. 65. **20 right:** AIC, Clarence Buckingham Collection, 1925.2409. **23, 25:** AIC, Helen Birch Bartlett Memorial Collection, 1928.610. **24:** AIC, bequest of Kate L. Brewster, 1949.263. **26:** AIC, gift of Mr. and Mrs. B. E. Bensinger, 1972.1167. **27:** AIC, Margaret Day Blake Collection, 1944.581. **28:** Getty Images / Taxi, AB08311. **30:** *Henri de Toulouse-Lautrec* (New York: Museum of Modern Art, 1985), p. 12.